Killers

A play

Adam Pernak

Samuel French — London
New York - Toronto - Hollywood

KILLERS

First produced at the Royal Court Theatre Upstairs,
London, on 13th November 1992 with the following
cast:

Jonathan Shand	Stephen McGann
David Shand	Mark McGann
Gerald	Jerome Willis
Marian	Madeline Blakeney
Mrs Shand	Rowena Cooper
Mr Shand	Sam Kelly
Veronica	Doon Mackichan
Trevor	Sam Kelly
Old Man	Jerome Willis
Waitress	Madeline Blakeney

Directed by Ian Rickson
Décor by Lucy Hall

COPYRIGHT INFORMATION

(See also page ii)

CHARACTERS

Jonathan Shand
David Shand
Gerald
Marian
Mrs Shand
Mr Shand
Veronica
Trevor
Old Man
Waitress

ACT I

ACT II

Time —— 1991

For Shirley, Jack and Dianne

USE OF OBLIQUES

An oblique (/) marks the point in a speech where the next speech overlaps, for example:

Mr Shand I'll tell you what it is. It's them bloody neighbours. That's what it is. You're only/doing it to get away from them.
Mrs Shand The neighbours have got nothing to do with it.

ACT I

A prison room

There is a table, slightly L, *and a chair to* L *of this. There is a door* R

The Lights come up brightly on Jonathan seated at the table. He rocks the chair back on to two legs and rests his feet on the edge of the table, knees bent, arms loose at his sides

There is the sound of the door being unlocked. The door opens and David enters. He edges tentatively into the room, stopping well short of the table. Jonathan rocks forward to his feet, slams his hands on the table and catches David with an ominously threatening glare

He moves around the table and up to David, close. A confused manner: he cannot decide whether David is here for good or bad reasons. His feelings towards David are deeply confused, fluctuating between his fraternal instincts and his newfound hostility

Jonathan You shouldn't be here. (*Pause*) We've got madmen here, a man to suit every ... (*He stops*) Why d'you come here? (*He looks at David*) You came to see what's happened. Well?

David is on the verge of replying, but cannot

You want to see what's happened? You want to see what's happened to me? Do you? I'll tell you, brother. (*Pause. He considers David cynically, angrily*) This is what I am now. OK? (*Angrily*) OK? (*Pause. He glares at David*) You think you know it all, think you did it. Maybe you think you did it better? Well I salute you, brother, (*he salutes*) but you didn't do a thing! You want to know about killing? I'll tell you about killing because you *clearly* don't know. (*He looks closely into David's face*) You hurt him. Close. Where he's soft and vulnerable. (*His hand to David's stomach, grabbing*) Get him, and watch. 'Cause you don't want to miss this.

Jonathan looks into David's eyes

His eyes. See the white. Hurt him, close, and the white — watch! — the white, it disappears. The pupil fills the eye. You know you've done enough when there's no more white. (*He smiles sickly and releases his grip*) Do you understand now?

Pause. David considers his brother, sadly. His expression penetrates Jonathan's façade

David I'm not going to lose you, Jonathan.

Jonathan is momentarily lost

Jonathan (*finally*) You bastard. (*He turn and moves away*) You didn't listen. You don't shit around with aeroplanes or bombs, you get close. You didn't see it. (*He rears on him angrily*) You didn't see it!

Pause

It's a game. You didn't realize? It's beautiful! (*He smiles*) No ... ?

Pause

(*Finally; angrily*) Bastard!

He turns and moves quickly, dismissively, to the far side of the room, L

Black-out

SCENE 1

The Shands' living-room

R, *a large table holds a buffet with a white iced cake as the centrepiece. It is a family party. Sprightly music*

The Lights come up on Mrs Shand emptying crisps into a bowl. Mr Shand sits in the armchair, L, engrossed in a model aeroplane he is constructing. Elsewhere, randomly seated around the room, are Gerald, Marian and Veronica. Their collective chatter, together with the music, generates a convivial party atmosphere

Gerald I want to drink a toast to him.

Marian He's not here yet.

Gerald He's a fine young man.

Mrs Shand Did someone call David?

Marian Wait till he gets here.

Gerald I like a tipple.

Marian So we can see.

Mrs Shand I think he's out in the garage. Will someone call David in — I want him in for when Jon gets here.

Gerald This wine tastes familiar. Is it a claret? It's very pungent. Tastes like my own stuff. Didn't I give you a couple of bottles last year?/Tastes familiar.

Mrs Shand I hope we all like cheese.

Gerald I've still got a couple left, haven't I?

Marian Yes, I think there's still a couple of dozen left.

Gerald Had to buy bulk, see. Had a bit of bother with the ingredients. I overdid the volumes.

Mrs Shand Yes, I'm sure we all like cheese. Look, will someone call David in.

Mr Shand Call him in yourself. You're not bloody mute, are you?

Veronica I'll go and fetch him.

Mrs Shand He's in the garage. Mind your frock.

Veronica exits

Mr Shand And tell him to wash his hands.

Mrs Shand He's twenty-eight.

Mr Shand I don't care. He still wants bloody watchin'.

Gerald I think mine had more of a punch to it.

Marian What are you going on about? (*To Mrs Shand*) They don't get any easier once they're older, do they?

Mrs Shand (*surveying the buffet*) I never know if I've made enough.

Marian There's plenty.

Mrs Shand I hope so. You like cheese, don't you, Marian?

Marian It's lovely. A nice cake.

Mrs Shand It's shop bought. I've been busy ...

Marian He's done ever so well though, hasn't he? A company car.

Mrs Shand It's only a small one. Ford Fiesta.

Marian Still. A company car, at twenty-five. It would've been unheard of. He has done well.

Mrs Shand He's always worked hard.

Marian He's a clever boy. They both are. They've both of them done you proud, Jean.

Mrs Shand smiles, looks across at Mr Shand, who remains engrossed in his model

Gerald There's wrestling on this afternoon. (*He lunges at the TV*) Can I just check? (*He tries to switch it on. Nothing happens*) What's happened? Is it broken?

Mrs Shand Won't it work? Oh dear. Are you sure it's plugged in?

Gerald checks

Marian You don't have to watch TV, dear. There is company. (*She indicates for him to sit down*)

Mrs Shand Maybe there's a wire loose. (*She tries the switch: no response*) That's strange. (*To Mr Shand*) Do you know what's wrong with it?

Mr Shand Broken.

Mrs Shand Well we can see that. Can't you do anything?

Mr Shand Been broken all week.

Mrs Shand Why didn't you say so?

Mr Shand Nowt worth watchin'. Bloody waste of time.

Mrs Shand If that's the case, I don't know why we bother having it standing there.

Mr Shand Sell it, then. Doesn't bother me.

Gerald You want to get it seen to. Don't be bothered with no guarantees. You've got your statutory rights. I know the man. A very good mate of mine, he's a sparky. He'd have a look at it, he'd have the back off. No problem.

Veronica enters

Mrs Shand We really ought to do something about it. (*To Veronica*) Did you tell him?

Veronica He's just finishing off.

Mrs Shand All these things, all going wrong. I don't have the patience. Anything electrical. If it's not the drier it's the wireless. And this thing's quite new. We only got it last year.

Gerald It's the durability, you see. When I worked, you built the thing to last. Now it's all material. If it looks good in the shops. Doesn't matter if it breaks down once it's home — got to look good in the shops.

Veronica Don't you work any more?

Gerald What's that?

Veronica You don't work any more?

Gerald Nah. It's my leg, you see. You see that? Here — feel that. (*He grabs her hand, touches his thigh with it*) Solid.

Veronica (*uneasily*) Yes.

Gerald It's been like that now — six years. That right?

Marian Yes. Six years.

Gerald Doctors? They don't wanna know. You get on a waiting list, they don't wanna know. I'm an invalid. Only a matter of time before I'm round an' about in one of them little green cars.

Veronica I didn't realize you were so bad.

Gerald Oh yes. I'm bad. I'm very bad. Oh yes.

Mrs Shand (*to Veronica*) Do you know how long I've known Marian?

Veronica shakes her head

(*Victoriously*) Forty-five years.

Veronica Really.

Mrs Shand Forty-five years. Her father had the toffee shop on our street.

Marian I used to steal you toffee chews. Do you remember?

Mrs Shand Do I remember! Course I do. She hid them down her sock. They used to melt.

Marian I had chocolate feet.

They laugh

David enters

David Hallo, hallo — someone's been at the sherry!

Mrs Shand Don't be cheeky.
Marian Hallo, David.
David Hallo, Marian.

He nods across at Gerald who lifts his glass

Mrs Shand (*to Mr Shand*) David's here. Come on, put your toys away.

Mr Shand reluctantly clears his models away

(*To David*) Did you fix it, David?
David I thought I had, but there's some pieces left over. I must've done something wrong.
Mrs Shand Don't you know what's wrong with it?
David Yes; it won't go.
Mrs Shand Go away! (*She swipes at him with a tea-towel*)
Gerald A very good mate of mine, he's got a garage. Barney's Repair Shop. You won't get a job done cheaper. Mention my name. He'll see you right.
Mrs Shand Jonathan's good with cars and things.
Gerald You want to ask for Barney.
David I know what I'm doing.
Mrs Shand He sorted it out last time.
David (*firmly*) Mum — I know what I'm doing.
Mrs Shand (*a little put out*) All right. Please yourself.

Slight pause

Marian You'll be getting off back soon. Back to Germany. Is it long yet?
David It's hard to say. A lot depends on this business in the Gulf.
Marian Oh yes, there's that, isn't there.
Gerald You hoping to see some action, David?
David Might not come to that.
Gerald You want to get out there. See a bit of action. It don't do a young man any harm to see a bit of the world. I wish I'd had your chances.
Marian You did your National Service.
Gerald Not the same thing. There's gonna be a war out there soon. There's gonna be heroes, real armed combat. We didn't have none of that.
Marian And a good thing too.

Gerald No; it's experience. It's seeing a part of life. If I didn't have this leg, I'd be making enquiries myself.

Mrs Shand (*to Mr Shand*) Come on, look sharpish — get that bottle of wine out.

He gets up, with reluctance, and moves to the sideboard

Gerald What's wrong with this?

Mrs Shand We've got a special bottle we're saving.

Gerald This stuff's good enough.

Mr Shand takes a bottle from the sideboard and hands it to his wife

Mrs Shand We have special bottles for special occasions. When was the last time? (*She starts to think*)

Marian I didn't realize you'd be making such a thing of it. We'd've made more of an effort.

David It doesn't matter.

Mrs Shand David joining the Air Force. That was the last time. Six years ago.

David More like eight.

Mrs Shand Is that how long it is? Doesn't time fly.

David (*changing the music*) Is that a pun?

Mrs Shand Eh?

Marian We had a party when Gerald was made redundant. I can't think why, he was miserable as sin about it.

Mrs Shand I don't know where the years go to, I really don't. It doesn't seem five minutes since they were little kids.

Marian I suppose the last happy occasion was when I passed my driving test.

Mrs Shand I struggle to keep up sometimes.

Marian It's four years since; at least that.

Gerald If we don't eat soon I'm going home.

Marian Don't be rude — we're waiting for Jonathan.

Gerald He's probably down the pub with his mates.

Mrs Shand David, what's this music?

David Don't you like it?

Mrs Shand It's different, I suppose.

David (*to Veronica*) You're quiet.

Veronica I've nothing to say.

Brief silence

Mrs Shand Ah, now then— what's this? (*She moves to the* L *window, and looks out*)
Marian Is it him?
Gerald (*standing*) Let's get started on this food, shall we? (*He moves to the table*)
Mrs Shand It's Jonathan! Now are we going to sing for him?
David It's not his birthday.
Mrs Shand It's still a celebration. (*She hits her husband on the head*) Come on, look sharpish. Let's make a thing of it.

Mr Shand stands, slowly, reluctantly. Gerald is helping himself to food

Marian Gerald! Wait till he gets here.
Gerald (*embarrassed*) All right.
Mr Shand What do you want me to do?
Mrs Shand Well, you might look happy for a start.

Mr Shand forces a grin which sits unhappily with him

Here he is!

The door L *opens. Jonathan enters*

Surprise! (*She points at the dinner table and cake*)

She rushes forward to hug Jonathan victoriously. He is embarrassed and plays along reluctantly

Jonathan Hallo, Mum! (*He looks up*) Oh, what's this? Are we having a party?
Mrs Shand Gerald and Marian came round.

They wave at him

I told them about ... well, I can mention it? Is it settled then?
Jonathan I think so.
Mrs Shand Oh, Jonathan! (*She hugs him again*)

Gerald takes the opportunity to help himself to the food

We're so proud of you!

Gerald This calls for a celebration. (*He takes a huge bite of sandwich*)

Mrs Shand Proud, proud, proud!

Marian Well done, Jonathan.

Jonathan It's not such a big thing.

Mrs Shand Don't be silly now. Head of a department at twenty-five. You don't get that handed to you on a plate.

Marian He is looking smart.

Jonathan takes his coat off as the rest start on the buffet. He deliberately looks to Veronica, whose smile is slightly subdued

Mrs Shand It's his best suit.

David (*shaking hands*) Well done.

Gerald Can I propose a toast now?

Mrs Shand (*handing him the bottle*) Here — why don't you open this.

Marian We've been hearing all about it. It's very exciting, isn't it. A company car and your own office.

Jonathan You want to see the office — it's like working in a shoe box.

Marian (*laughing*) Oh, really!

Mrs Shand He's always been a modest lad. Never one to lap up the praise.

Jonathan (*quietly, to David*) This is nice, isn't it.

David Gerald's totally gone. He's tanked up on that plonk of his.

Jonathan A taste of his own medicine.

Gerald (*struggling with the bottle*) What's going on? Did you weld this thing on?

Marian I like these glasses./ Are they new?

David He'd drink anything you gave/ him. Anything he could lay his hands on.

Mrs Shand No; we've had them donkey's years.

Jonathan Good thing the goldfish died.

They laugh

Mrs Shand Come on now, boys, what's the joke?

Jonathan Oh Mother, what a lovely cake!

Mrs Shand The cake! I forgot. Wait a minute, everyone. (*She searches for the matches, finds them, lights the candle on the cake*)

Mr Shand (*waving a sandwich at no-one in particular*) Is this cheese? It's on t' turn.

Marian (*to Gerald*) What's the matter? Can't you do it?

Gerald I've got it. A glass! Come on now — a glass. That's it.

Gerald pours the wine. Marian hands it round as he pours

   Now this is special wine, see,/ 'cause it's a special occasion.

Jonathan is handed a glass, which he passes on to Veronica

Jonathan You all right?
Veronica I wish people would stop asking me that. I'll end up with/ a complex. Don't I look all right?
Marian Just a small glass for me, dear.
Jonathan You look fine.
Veronica Fine. That's nice.
Mrs Shand Are these trick candles? They won't take.
Jonathan I rang last night.
Gerald (*loudly*) Pass/ 'em round. Come on then.
Veronica I was asleep.
Jonathan I know.
Gerald One each.
Veronica So ...?

He shrugs

Mrs Shand All right, everyone. Jonathan. Let's have you to the front, please, to blow out your candles.
Jonathan Oh blimey!
David Come on then ——
Gerald That's right.
David — big puff!
Marian It is a nice cake.
Mr Shand Cheese is off.
Jonathan (*hamming*) Really, Mother, for me? You shouldn't have.
Mrs Shand Come on!

He blows out the candles. Sporadic applause, weak cheers

Jonathan Do I make a wish?
Mrs Shand Cut the cake.
David It's got wax on it.

Mrs Shand No it hasn't.

Gerald I'd like to propose a toast.

Marian Wait till they've done the cake.

Mrs Shand Is everyone having cake? Veronica?

Veronica Just a small piece for me.

Gerald A toast, to a fine young man. To Jonathan!

Gerald raises his glass. No-one else does. He lowers his glass, mumbling, disgruntled

Marian You're not doing it even.

Mr Shand Hey, I'll have a bigger piece than that — I paid for t' bugger!

Mrs Shand Don't push — you'll all get a piece.

David moves to sit in the R armchair. Jonathan follows and sits on the settee. During the following, the rest continue to chatter in the background

David You've done well.

Jonathan shrugs

 Is it not what you wanted?

Jonathan More or less. The office is a bit small,/ the money's good.

[**Marian** I'm not too fond of paper plates, but they serve their purpose, don't they.]

David Not bad. Is that what you asked for/

[**Mrs Shand** They do.]

Jonathan About that. A bit more, actually. I'm not complaining.

David What's up with Veronica? She's quiet.

Jonathan Is she?

[**Mrs Shand** I was tempted to get the china out, but I'm always on pins for breakages.]

David Haven't you noticed?

Jonathan I've hardly seen her.

[**Mrs Shand** It's not so much the lads/ I'm bothered about — I've got to keep my eye on (*nodding at Mr Shand*)him .]

Jonathan D'you get the car fixed?

Gerald starts to move behind the settee

[**Marian** I'm the same with him. Oh,/ he's off again!]
David Almost.
[**Marian** Up to no good!]
Jonathan Was it the plugs?
David I don't know.
Jonathan Didn't you try them?
David I don't think it is the plugs.
Jonathan Didn't you try them?
David No. You're not always right, you know. Why don't you talk to Veronica?

Jonathan glares at him, as Gerald moves between them and sits beside Jonathan

Gerald What's this then, eh — boy's talk?
Jonathan How are you keeping, Gerald? I haven't seen you for a while.
Gerald It's not good. There's not a lot they can do. You see that? (*He indicates his thigh*) It's tightened solid now.

Marian and Mrs Shand watch his performance, exchanging the occasional glance, singularly unimpressed

Like that (*he clenches his fist*) — you see? Can't move it. I wake up some mornings, I can't get out of bed.
Jonathan David's like that most mornings.
Gerald It's not good. It's been giving me some grief, I can tell you. You ask Marian — she'll tell you. I've been very bad. I'm not a well man.
Marian (*obediently*) He's not.
Jonathan (*mischievously*) Do you think you'll ever work again?

Gerald shakes his head slowly, soberly, his eyes closed

Gerald I shall be lucky to see another day's work. It's a travesty. Very sad. There's an answer I always give when people ask me that question.

David and Jonathan smile at each other knowingly

Specialists told me I'd never work again,/

[**Marian** (*extending her empty glass*) Would you, Jean?]

Mrs Shand tops up the glass

Gerald but they don't know everything and they can be wrong. A lot of great men struggled against the odds. And the reason/
[**Marian** (*to Mrs Shand*) Thank you, dear.]

Mrs Shand moves across the room, playing the hostess: a bottle of wine in one hand, a plate of sandwiches in the other

Gerald they succeeded was 'cause they never gave up. You see, they never gave up. (*Dramatic pause*) Never say die.

David and Jonathan mouth "Never say die" along with him

Jonathan It's a brave philosophy.
Mr Shand There's wax on this cake. Can you see that? Wax.
Mrs Shand (*impatiently*) Wipe it off with your fork. Don't make such a scene! Come on, Veronica — there's not enough there to fill a sparrow. Have some more sandwiches. You like cheese, don't you?
Veronica This is plenty, thank you.
Mrs Shand Come on. (*She places a couple more sandwiches on Veronica's plate*)
Marian We were listening to the radio coming over here and they said that there'd be an economic recession if we went to war. It's not looking good, is it.
Jonathan They might still give sanctions a bit longer.
Gerald It's gonna be war. There's no doubt about it. (*To David*) I don't mean to scare you, but they're not going to give it much longer before they get in there to fight it out. It's gonna be bad.

Jonathan stands and moves over to Veronica

Marian Well you might not be so gloomy.
Gerald It's an opinion.
Marian Maybe David doesn't want to hear your opinion.
Gerald He's got it anyway. (*He bites into a sandwich*)
Jonathan (*quietly, to Veronica*) I need to talk to you.
Marian (*to Gerald*) Watch your crumbs!

Veronica We'll talk later.

Jonathan That's what I mean — later. We can't talk now.

Mrs Shand (*overhearing*) Hurry up with your lunches everyone. I thought we might go out for a walk, before it goes dark.

Marian When will we get to see Reg's famous allotment?

Mrs Shand Well, Reg?

Mr Shand I'll take you later. It's no secret.

Gerald I shall have to give you some tips on radishes. I've grown radishes that've won prizes.

Mr Shand I do all right with radishes.

Gerald Oh no, you wanna see mine. Big ripe radishes. I say so myself, I never saw a better radish than the ones I used to grow.

Mrs Shand Don't you grow them any more?

Gerald Well, it's the leg, see. I can't bend.

Mrs Shand Of course.

Gerald Else I'd still be growing them. It's the leg.

Slight pause

Marian (*looking at Jonathan and Veronica*) They do make a lovely couple, don't they?

Gerald (*glancing at his watch*) Shame your telly won't work — it's darts on now.

Marian Are we going to see a nice wedding soon?

Both smile at her, clearly looking to avoid answering

Mrs Shand They've only been together two years. There's plenty of time yet.

Marian It's the perfect time, though. What with Jonathan's new job. Do you like shopping, Veronica?

Veronica smiles back

Lovely girl.

Mrs Shand We've always said that we'll help them out financially. We can't do much with Reg out of work but the house is all paid for now and we've got a bit put by. (*Irritated*) David, do you think we could have some more music?

David More music? As well as this?

Mrs Shand It's very loud. How about something more classy?

David OK. (*He changes the music*)

Mrs Shand I try to be with-it, I follow the hit parade, but some of it does get a bit on the loud side.

Mr Shand (*putting his plate on the coffee table*) Nice cake that. Where d'you get it?

Mrs Shand Listen to that. Something suits! Wonders'll never cease.

Veronica I said I'd be home for half-past six.

Jonathan It's not even six yet.

Veronica I know. I just thought I'd tell you.

Mrs Shand Help yourself to the buffet everyone.

David (*referring to music*) Is this any better?

Mrs Shand Much better.

Gerald Is there any more wine?

Marian I think you've had enough.

Gerald I was only making enquiries.

Mr Shand starts to put his shoes on

Mrs Shand What are you doing?

Mr Shand Thought you said you wanted to see the allotment.

Mrs Shand Are you going now?

Mr Shand It'll be dark soon.

Mrs Shand You could wait while we're finished.

Mr Shand I've finished.

Mrs Shand Well the rest of us might not have.

Mr Shand I'll go on ahead. I've some tidying up to do. (*He stands*)

Mrs Shand Please yourself. He's a mind of his own at times.

Gerald I think I'll come with you.

Mr Shand There's no need.

Gerald (*standing*) I'd just as soon set off now. Give me a better chance with my leg. If you don't mind walking slowly.

Marian Be careful on that pavement. Don't forget, you've been drinking.

Gerald All right.

Marian (*to Mrs Shand*) It's so embarrassing. Ever since I learned to drive, he's been drinking like a fish. And he can't hold it, he really can't.

Gerald I heard that. I can hold my own as good as any man.

Marian We'll see when the cold air gets you.

Gerald I'll be all right. No problem.

Mr Shand and Gerald exit

Jonathan Do you/ want to go for a walk?
Marian (*inevitably*) He'll fall again.
Veronica Not really.
Jonathan We need to talk.
Mrs Shand We'll set off in a minute. You'll have the house to yourselves.
David I've got the car to finish off.
Mrs Shand Aren't you coming with us?
David I've seen the allotment a million times.
Marian Oh, do come with us, David. It might be the last chance I get to see you ... (*correcting herself, embarrassed*) this time, I mean.
David I suppose I could walk you to the end.

Jonathan pours himself a glass of wine

Marian It's a long time since I went walking with a handsome young man. Are you sure you don't want to go and put your uniform on?

David smiles

Mrs Shand He's very smart in his uniform. Have I shown you the pictures?
David Yes, I think you have, Mum.
Mrs Shand Did I, Marian?
Marian Yes — I think you did.
Mrs Shand Oh. (*She sniffs, slightly put out*)
Jonathan I don't mean to be pushy at all, but if you're going ...
Mrs Shand All right. We know how to take a hint.

They move to the R door

We'll be over at the allotments if you need anything.
Veronica Thanks for the meal, Mrs Shand.
Mrs Shand We'll see you later, won't we?
Veronica I need to be home in half an hour.
Mrs Shand Oh, I see. As I say, Jonathan, we're at the allotments if you need us.
Marian See you later.
Jonathan 'Bye.

Marian Bye-bye.
Jonathan Yes.
Mrs Shand See you later.
Jonathan (*impatiently*) Yes.
David Bye-bye.
Marian Bye-bye.
Veronica Bye-bye.
Jonathan Goodbye.

David, Marian and Mrs Shand exit

Jonathan turns the music off. There is an uneasy silence for several seconds

Well?
Veronica Very good.
Jonathan Is that it?
Veronica I said congratulations. I said I was pleased for you.
Jonathan Did you?

Pause. He drinks up. During the following, he pours a couple of glasses of wine and gives one to Veronica

It makes things easier now. Eighteen thousand. Did I tell you, that's what I'm on?

She nods

It's quite a difference. And a car. We're mobile now. No more borrowing David's old thing. A brand new car. Are you all right?
Veronica Yes.
Jonathan (*excitedly*) It's the promotion! It's what we've been waiting for. This is it. I can move out of here, get a mortgage. We can get ourselves started. I tell you, I was talking to Darren — you know Darren: big, tall, blond lad, moustache, works in accounts — about the property boom, and he says there's going to be another boom, and this time it could be even bigger. Only this time, we're going to be in on it! (*He chuckles*) I tell you, this is going to be big.

She smiles. Pause

We've got to celebrate. Do you want to see a show? Go for a meal? I'll
book us a table. Shall we do that? A meal and a show? All right?

Veronica All right.

Jonathan We've got to tell people. Did you tell your parents?

Veronica I mentioned it.

Jonathan Were they pleased?

Veronica Well, I couldn't tell them for definite ——

Jonathan Of course — only found out today. Still, they'll be pleased
when we tell them. Do you realize I'm the youngest manager in the
whole company? Did you know that? Danny Lloyd's the next — he's
twenty-seven. Twenty-seven, married, his wife's just had their third kid.
Can you believe that!

Pause

Veronica Jonathan, do you mind if I go home?

Jonathan Aren't you feeling well?

Veronica I want to go home.

Jonathan All right. (*He stands*) Are you tired?

No reply. An ominous silence

Veronica.

She looks at him guiltily

What's going on?

She looks down, upset

What happened last night?

Veronica Nothing.

Jonathan I called your house.

Veronica Didn't Mum tell you, I went to bed.

Jonathan We'd arranged to meet.

No reply

Were you with someone?

Veronica (*too sharply*) No!

Jonathan I don't believe you. Who was it?

Pause

Veronica (*uncomfortably*) Look, will you drive me home.
Jonathan I want to know about this.

She tries to stand. He pushes her back

Veronica Jonathan ...! (*She tries again*) Jonathan ...! Get off, will you.
Jonathan Tell me what's going on.
Veronica Nothing ...!

He leans in front of her, determinedly. In submission, she starts to cry

Jonathan What happened?
Veronica It wasn't his fault.
Jonathan What wasn't?

She is crying

   Who was it? Veronica ...
Veronica It all got out of hand.
Jonathan Veronica ... Will you tell me — who were you with?

A pause. She is crying. He holds her tightly

Veronica (*softly*) Trevor.
Jonathan Trevor? That friend of your dad's?
Veronica Oh Jonathan? Don't get angry ...!
Jonathan Why? What happened?

Pause

   Did he touch you? (*Definitely*) He touched you.

She shakes her head to mean 'No' but is clearly lying

   This is disgusting.

A moment; he turns and moves to exit L

Veronica No! Jonathan — please!

Jonathan (*defiantly*) I'm sorting this out!
Veronica Don't!

Jonathan exits L

Veronica cries

Fade to Black-out

SCENE 2

The same. Night

The room is in near darkness

Mrs Shand sits in an armchair, a mug of tea in one hand, a half-eaten sandwich on a plate on her lap. She stares blankly ahead. She is dressed in night clothes

David enters R, also in night clothes. He sits in L seat of the settee

David I got my posting.
Mrs Shand I know.
David How did you know?

Silence

Mrs Shand It'll give you experience.

No reply

Didn't you always say you were bored with round here? That there's no future.
David This is different.
Mrs Shand How is it?
David It's different. (*Pause*) You mustn't worry.
Mrs Shand Oh, no fear of that. You're big enough now. I won't be worrying — I gave up worrying a long time ago.

David smiles, he knows her too well

Do you know they're calling it a war now? It gives me shivers. I never
thought it'd come to this.

David Don't you think it's quite exciting?

Mrs Shand I never thought we'd see another war. I feel so helpless. You
know, it gets me so angry. That I can't do anything. Do you know what
I mean?

David What could you be expected to do?

Mrs Shand That's just it. The likes of me. We have to just sit back and
accept it. There's nothing we can do about it. We can write to the MP.
I don't even know who he is. It's ridiculous.

Pause

How do we get ourselves involved in these things?

David What?

Mrs Shand You going out there.

David You know why. I have to.

Mrs Shand You have to. Why doesn't everyone else have to? It doesn't
seem right. Why should it have to be us with the worry?

Pause

David I'm sorry.

Mrs Shand Oh, nothing for you to be sorry for. You never did a thing in
your life that you didn't think was right. There's nothing for you to be
sorry for. We shall just have to be brave.

Pause

You will be careful?

David What do you think?

Mrs Shand Because I still can't think of you as a grown man. You're still
a responsibility to me. You do see that? I feel so terrible about this.

David Mum!

He takes her hand. She becomes tearful

Mrs Shand Don't look at me, David. It's bad enough as it is. Oh, I'm a
disgrace. (*She wipes her eyes and sniffs*) David, can't you do something?

David Such as what?

Mrs Shand I don't know. Something. Anything. Is there nothing you can do?

David It's my job.

Mrs Shand Oh, your job. What's a job? They can't force you.

David They can.

Mrs Shand But they wouldn't. You could tell them you were sick.

David No I can't.

Mrs Shand Tell them you're deranged. You can't control a fighter plane in a state like that.

David Mother, I'm not going to tell them I'm deranged. I'm not going to tell them anything.

Pause

It's my duty. I have to do it.

Mrs Shand But the circumstances...

David I know what I'm doing.

Mrs Shand It's dangerous.

David I know that it's dangerous.

Mrs Shand David.

David Mother — I know that it's dangerous. I know what it involves. I don't need you to tell me.

Mrs Shand Oh, I see.

David I'm sorry. But it's true.

Pause

You'll be OK, won't you?

Silence

You'll be all right — you and Dad?

She tuts in disgust

What?

Mrs Shand Don't mention him.

David Why?

Mrs Shand Don't mention him.

David What's he done?

Mrs Shand He thinks it's marvellous. He's all for it. We were watching

it, the other night. They were debating on whether it was all necessary.
" 'Course it's necessary!" your dad says, "we've got to show them
who's boss. We'll not take no hassle from no bloody foreigners." He
shook his fist, he got very emotional about it. "Wait till my lad gets out
there! He'll lay into them, he'll show them not to mess! Wait while my
lad gets to them!"

David laughs

He was serious. He really does believe that. He thinks you're going to
get out there, single-handedly win this war for us. That's how he's
thinking.

David He doesn't mean anything.

Mrs Shand He does. He's not like me. We're different.

Pause

When do you go?

David Wednesday.

Mrs Shand This Wednesday?

David Yes.

Mrs Shand This Wednesday?

He nods. Pause

It's a long way.

Pause

What's the procedure — do they fly you there?

David Yes.

Mrs Shand Do you need anything? You must tell us if you need anything.

David They gave me a basic list.

Mrs Shand Toothbrush, toilet rolls ...

David There's a list.

Mrs Shand Anything at all. Tell me — if you need it. (*Pause. She stands
and moves to the* L *window*) What time is it? (*She looks at her watch*) Oh,
look at it!

David Are you waiting up for Jonathan?

Mrs Shand Heavens, God forbid! (*Slight pause*) He should be in by now.

David He's celebrating.

Mrs Shand He still should be in.
David He'll be with his friends.
Mrs Shand He didn't ring me. He usually rings.
David He'll be with Veronica.

She shakes her head, makes a disparaging noise

   What?
Mrs Shand They had an argument.
David Did they? When? What about?
Mrs Shand I don't know. She didn't say.
David She rang you?
Mrs Shand I rang her.
David When was this? What did she say?
Mrs Shand Not much. Just that they argued. He's angry, of course. He
   went off somewhere.
David You think he might be in trouble?
Mrs Shand I don't know. Do you want this sandwich?

She offers him the plate. He takes the sandwich

   Is your father still snoring?
David Like a pig.

She tuts

   Listen, what did Veronica say? I thought he was going to talk to her.
Mrs Shand He'll be so upset.
David I know.
Mrs Shand Poor boy! Oh David, what's happening? I'm in such a state.
David It's probably nothing.

She looks at him

   Look, if he's not back in half an hour, I'll have a drive round.
Mrs Shand I'm annoyed with myself for worrying. It's so silly. (*She
   stands*) I ought to go to sleep. (*Pause*) David, I wish you didn't have to
   go. Why don't you think about it, eh?
David I've thought about it.
Mrs Shand Think again.

She looks at him, he looks away

She takes the plate and mug and moves resignedly into the kitchen and switches on the light

David I was going to show you the letter, I got it yesterday. It was so official. It read like an order.
Mrs Shand (*off*) It is an order.
David I couldn't believe it. It made me go numb. For about an hour. I couldn't believe it. We've been told to listen to loud aggressive music, to psyche us up. And we chant things. Like football chants.

Pause

I can't believe it's the real thing. All this acting, pretending, and now ...

Mrs Shand emerges from the kitchen

Mrs Shand Are you saying something?

He shakes his head

She returns to the kitchen

David Better than training exercises, I suppose. I get so sick of them. "Here are your weapons. Here are your bearings. This is the enemy. Your task: to destroy the enemy targets." It's like a game.

The kitchen light goes off

Mrs Shand returns

They are silent

Mrs Shand (*with forced optimism*) We'll be all right as long as you are.

No reply. She moves to leave

David Mum ... I was never so scared in all my life.

Fade to Black-out

SCENE 3

The street. Evening

Jonathan stands by a gate to a house driveway. He wears his suit from Act I, Scene 1, his hands firmly rooted into his pockets. He moves slightly, impatiently, looking about him. Finally, noticing the approach of some-one, he straightens himself, poises himself to speak

Trevor enters L. He is a short, middle-aged man. He walks with his head down and approaches the gate. He stops when Jonathan blocks his way

Jonathan Trevor.
Trevor (*warily*) Yeah? (*Pause*) Who are you? (*Pause*) Here, I know you. You're the bloke ——
Jonathan Jonathan.
Trevor Yeah, that's it. Jonathan. Used to be seein' Colin's girl.
Jonathan Veronica.
Trevor Yeah. Nice girl. (*Slight pause*) You all right then, Jonathan? I mean, what you doin' here?
Jonathan I've come to see you. I want to talk to you.
Trevor Ahh, right. What's up, then? What's the matter?
Jonathan I want to ask you something. (*Directly*) You and Veronica — what's going on?

Pause. Trevor laughs, uncomfortably

Trevor Dunno what you mean.
Jonathan (*angrily*) I mean last night. Come on, Trevor — what've you been up to?
Trevor (*shaking his head*) This is well out of order. What's your problem, mate?
Jonathan You're the problem — mate. You leave her alone.

He glares at Trevor who smirks, cockily

D'you hear me?

Trevor laughs, shakes his head

Trevor Nice girl, Veronica. Don't know what she's doin' with a yuppie bastard like you.

Jonathan squares up to him

Get out of it! (*He pushes Jonathan*) Piss off!

Jonathan stands his ground, unsure of what to do, but determined not to let Trevor past

Jonathan I hate you so much. I don't know what you did to her, but you're going to pay.

He makes a fist, but Trevor gets in first and pushes Jonathan firmly back. Jonathan rushes at him and hits him in the stomach. Trevor falls back on to the floor. Jonathan stands over him

You leave her alone. Don't go near her ever again. If you go near her again, I'll kill you.

As he turns to leave, Trevor staggers to his feet and lunges at Jonathan. He punches him in the back of the head. Jonathan staggers to his knees. Trevor continues to hit and kick him as Jonathan struggles to shield the blows. Eventually he turns and, in the struggle, lands a blow which forces Trevor back. Trevor stops fighting, a worried look on his face. Jonathan stops and stands, scared

Trevor clasps at his chest, lunging for breath. He is coughing and spluttering, writhing with pain. Jonathan reaches forward, but can do nothing but watch. Then Trevor collapses on to the floor, his struggling becomes less, then he is still. Jonathan stands for a moment, horrified. He starts to panic as the true severity of the situation registers. He is very scared. He stares at Trevor's motionless body, helpless

Then he turns and, in a panic, runs off

Fade to Black-out

28 Killers

SCENE 4

An outdoor café in the park. Morning

There are two white tables with chairs

Birdsong. A rich blue light comes up

At the table UR *sits an old man in a rumpled suit, tie, and polished shoes. He mumbles to himself and the Waitress as she wipes his table clean*

Old Man They think they know what they're doin'. Think they're smart, rushin' in like that. Well we'll see about it.

Pause

Did you vote for 'em? Did you?
Waitress No.
Old Man No. Exactly. I've not met a single person what did. Not one. Meant to be a democracy. Who votes for 'em? Who? I'd like to know.

Pause

We'll 'ave an invasion next, you mark my words. We'll be down in bunkers, like the last time. It's in the air.

Pause

Did I tell you about the bird? I saw a bird — a sparrow — just fly into a sheet of glass. Didn't notice it, just flew straight into it. Smashed its face in, fell to t' floor — dead.

Veronica enters L. *She wears a dark winter coat, possibly a hat. She looks about her then sits at* L *table*

You see things are happening, things we can't explain. It's a bad air, bad moods. It's leading to something, I can tell.

The Waitress moves across to Veronica's table

Waitress Yes, love.

Veronica thinks

Veronica Coffee, please. Black, no sugar.
Waitress (*noting it down*) Coffee, black. Anything to eat?
Veronica No. That's all, thank you.
Waitress Thank you.

The Waitress pockets her pad and pen and exits R

Veronica unbuttons her coat, removes her hat, straightens her hair, looking off to L

Old Man They've got nuclear weapons.

She looks over at him

We want to keep out of it. We're far too keen, that's our problem. They'll blow us — an' then where will we be.

She smiles, kindly, but looks away again

There's only so much you can ignore. Ignoring things won't make them go away. They'll fester in t' corner. They'll get worse.

Pause

We're goin' to wake up one morning, an' it's goin' to be dark. No sunrise — dark. The sun'll've forgotten to come up. Why's that? Maybe it'll just give up hope. (*He pauses, contemplatively, pleased with his profundity*)

Mrs Shand enters L. *She approaches the table slowly, stands*

The two women consider each other silently for a time

Mrs Shand (*finally, duteously*) Hallo.
Veronica (*encouragingly*) Hallo.

Pause. Veronica laughs, embarrassed

I'm sorry. Sit down.

A moment, then Mrs Shand sits

Thank you.
Mrs Shand What for?
Veronica For coming.
Mrs Shand Oh.

Pause. Mrs Shand looks about her

It's very quiet.
Veronica (*eagerly*) Yes.
Mrs Shand Very nice, though.
Veronica It is, yes.
Mrs Shand I'm curious to know, why did you choose here?
Veronica I'm sorry?
Mrs Shand You were very precise. You said, "In the park, the café. First
table on the left."

No response. Veronica feels threatened

Old Man I heard sounds last night.
Mrs Shand (*to Veronica*) Ah well, I just wondered. (*She turns to look at
the Old Man*)
Old Man He says I'm deaf, but I heard them sounds as clear as a bell.
Thudding. Hammering. Like someone tryin' to escape. I had a look, but
I couldn't see anything. Too dark. But it was something. Or someone.
(*He falls silent*)
Mrs Shand (*turning back*) Funny man.
Veronica I'm sorry if I troubled you. I tried to think of who there was ...
I thought of you.

Slight pause

You were always kind. I could always talk to you. I always thought of
you as a friend.
Mrs Shand Things have happened.
Veronica I know.
Mrs Shand There's a lot changed.
Veronica I know. Mrs Shand — I want to just tell you, as someone who
knows him, that I ... didn't want any of this.
Mrs Shand I don't think any of us wanted any of this.
Veronica I've been very ill.

Pause

[**Old Man** Sometimes I hear music.]

Mrs Shand (*trying*) You can't even begin to realize ... He's a different boy.

[**Old Man** This constant thudding — boom, boom, boom.]

Mrs Shand (*uncomfortable*) Look, I don't know why I came here. I don't feel that it's right. (*She makes to leave*)

Veronica Please don't go! Mrs Shand, please! I really need to speak to you. I've got to tell you. (*Her hand to her face, pressing her temple*) I'm not well. I'm very tired.

[**Old Man** You daren't ask 'em.]

Veronica Mrs Shand, does he mention me?

Mrs Shand If you knew the state he's in, you wouldn't be asking that.

Veronica But does he mention me?

No reply

[**Old Man** They'd clobber you!]

Veronica I need to know. I still think of him, every day. Sometimes it's incessant. And I wish that I wouldn't, but I do. And I still love him. It's ridiculous ...! I'm trying so hard, to be how I should.

Pause

I want to see him. What I mean is, I want to speak to him. Just one last time.

Mrs Shand You mustn't try to see him.

Veronica Does he hate me?

Mrs Shand It's not that. All I'm saying is, for his sake, please ...

Veronica Just one last ...

Mrs Shand (*firmly*) No.

The Waitress returns with a cup of coffee

Waitress (*putting it down*) One cup of coffee. (*To Mrs Shand*) Anything else, love?

Mrs Shand No, thank you.

Waitress Thank you. (*She moves to leave*)

Old Man (*as she passes*) It's a dangerous nation.

Waitress (*not stopping*) It certainly is.

The Waitress exits R

Veronica It's strange, I don't feel sorry for Trevor, not at all, and he's dead. It's Jonathan I feel for, as if he were the victim. Isn't that strange!

Slight pause. The Old Man stands and starts to exit L

How is he?

A long, contemplative pause

Mrs Shand (*slowly*) He's lost. Confused. Sometimes — angry. He's frightened.
Veronica Will you give him this? (*She takes an audio-cassette from her pocket*) I haven't said what I wanted to say, because I can't. Not without seeing him. But I won't be seeing him. Please, Mrs Shand.

Mrs Shand takes the cassette

Thank you.

Pause

It's been difficult for me, this whole thing. I haven't spoken to anyone about it, (*she points to the cassette*) except Jonathan. Other people can't understand. I don't think *he* understood really. It would never have worked, him and me. He never really knew me. He thought he did. But we were never — together. I loved him, but it was never enough. What did he want? Why were things never enough?
Mrs Shand He was scared.
Veronica Scared? What was he scared of?

Pause

Mrs Shand Of who he might become. Weren't you ever scared of who you might become?

Pause. The two women look at each other

I should go now.
Veronica You will give it to him?
Mrs Shand Yes. (*She puts the cassette in her handbag and snaps it shut.*

She stands)
Veronica Mrs Shand. (*Pause*) I'm sorry. For everything.

Mrs Shand looks at her, but does not reply

Mrs Shand I'll give him the tape.

A moment. They consider each other: Veronica somewhat pathetically, vulnerably, looking up; Mrs Shand surely, fixed and determined

Then Mrs Shand exits L

The Lights fade to Black-out

SCENE 5

A spotlight comes up on Mrs Shand C. *A sombre expression. She starts to speak immediately*

Mrs Shand I picked up the phone. A voice said, "Mrs Shand?" I said yes. He said, "This is the Ministry of Defence." I said yes. He said, "I'm afraid we have some rather bad news for you." I went quiet. I knew straightaway what he meant. He said, "Mrs Shand?" I said, yes. He said, "I'm afraid I have some rather bad news about your son David." I was still quiet. I felt numb. I braced myself. I knew what was coming. He said, "I'm afraid David has been killed." He went quiet. I went quiet. I must have stood there, numb, for about fifteen seconds. I didn't know what to say. I forgot he was there. I just thought about David. I couldn't register anything. I just thought, "David." Then suddenly the man started to laugh. I froze. Then in the most disgusting, evil voice I ever heard he said, "Fooled you!" Then he hung up. That was it.

Black-out

CURTAIN

ACT II

SCENE 1

Mr Shand's allotment

L *Mr Shand digs the soil. In the far* R *corner, Mrs Shand is kneeling, not facing her husband, planting seeds*

Mr Shand You struggle to do right by 'em, an' this is what you get — grief. (*Pause*) Thing is, they've 'ad chances. I never 'ad chances. Me 'an' Dennis, we were never given leeway the way they were. We did what we were told. Didn't do us much 'arm. Well, not Dennis anyway. (*Slight pause*) An' 'e were never smarter than me. 'E always struggled. 'E were bloody stupid, best o' times. (*Slight pause*) What's 'e got? 'E's got 'ouse wi' a pool... 'E's got no mortgage... 'E's got two new cars ... a nice young wife. 'E's got black 'air for a start. (*Slight pause*) 'E were thick were Dennis. I did 'is homework for 'im. 'E were thick.

He continues digging, disgruntled. He stops

I should be more like Dennis. 'E does things right. Didn't get married till 'e'd done what 'e wanted. Even in 'ard times, when business were bad, 'e never let it bother 'im. I'm not like that. I'm too bloody soft; I let things bother me. I were too bloody soft wi' them lads. Now look what's 'appened. (*Slight pause*) D'you finish them carrots?
Mrs Shand I'm doing them.
Mr Shand Still doin' 'em? Bloody 'ell. Good job we started early. An' I hope we'll not 'ave that Gerald and Marian round again. They're bloody demented. They've got no sense. Well, Gerald hasn't. I don't like him.
Mrs Shand I know you don't know.
Mr Shand They come for one reason. They come to gloat; they love it. Gerald never liked me. He thinks it's all my fault. He doesn't think it's you; it's me. Bloody bugger. He better not come round — that's what I say. Are they your best trousers?
Mrs Shand No.

Mr Shand They used to be.
Mrs Shand Used to be. That was twenty years ago.
Mr Shand They used to be your best. There's nowt wrong with 'em.

She sits up and points to worn material on the knees

They'd patch up. What're you on about?

She resumes her work

You might not be so miserable.

No reply. He moves towards her

I say, you might not be so miserable.

Still no reply. He returns to his digging

Misery. You get on with it. You don't see me moping around. I get on with it. It's not pleasant, I know, but it's not going to go away. (*Slight pause*) What about the news — we could have David home soon. What about that?

No reply

You don't help yourself.

He digs some more

I spoke to that girl from t' paper. Did I tell you? She's sending us a copy. She was very nice. Quite a pretty lass. I told you, didn't I?
Mrs Shand I don't want to know about that.
Mr Shand Please yourself; I'm telling you anyway. We'll be five hundred quid better off for it. (*Slight pause*) I never 'ad money of me own. T' minute it came in it'd be back out again. There was always summat. I shouldn't have married young. Should've lived a bit. (*Slight pause*) I had three ambitions when I was their age. One was to be rich enough not to work. One was to go to America. One was to be happily married. I used to sit up at night and plan it out. I couldn't care less now. Nowt to do wi' me.

Mrs Shand You tell me not to be so miserable.

Mr Shand I don't know what I'd do if I won t' pools. What would you do? I'd go to America. I wouldn't tell anyone.

Mrs Shand Not even me?

Mr Shand I'd buy a big flash car. I'd drive up to that warehouse, hammer on Wilson's door, take him outside, I'd say, "Look at that! Sod you, Wilson. Don't need your soddin' job no more. Look at that." That's what I'd do.

Mrs Shand What good would that do you?

Mr Shand It'd show him.

Mrs Shand Oh. Well you'll have to win the pools then.

He stands for a moment, in poised defiance. Then he resumes digging

Mr Shand What would you do?

Mrs Shand What?

Mr Shand What would you do if we came up?

Mrs Shand Oh, I don't know. I don't think I'd care. I'd give it away.

Mr Shand I'll not tell you if I win.

Mrs Shand I don't think money matters. Not in the way they think it matters. It's all right if you've got it, I suppose. Even if you've got it, there'll always be something.

Mr Shand Misery.

Silence

I had another of them phone calls earlier. It's not as often now.

Mrs Shand What did he say?

Mr Shand More of the same. Said I was evil. Evil, death and Satan. "Death to you all!" he said. "Bugger off!" I said. I put t' phone down. He never called back. (*Suddenly*) What are you doin' with them carrots?

Mrs Shand What? I'm doin' what you said.

Mr Shand I didn't say there.

Mrs Shand You did.

Mr Shand I didn't. I said there for t' carrots. (*He points*) You should be doin' them over there.

Mrs Shand What's wrong with here?

Mr Shand They'll get no sun there. It's useless there. I told you.

Mrs Shand Sorry. What shall I do?

Mr Shand How many have you done?

Mrs Shand All of them.

Mr Shand All of them! Bloody 'ell. I said there. Didn't you hear me?

Mrs Shand (*a little upset*) No. I've been doing them for a half an hour, you should've told me.

Mr Shand I didn't know what you were doing.

Mrs Shand I asked you if they were right, you said they were.

Mr Shand I didn't.

Mrs Shand You did.

Mr Shand You must've asked me summat else.

Mrs Shand What shall I do with them?

He thinks

Mr Shand Might as well leave 'em. We might get a few.

Mrs Shand I can dig them up.

Mr Shand Just leave 'em.

She stands and wipes the soil from her hands

Mrs Shand I'm sorry.

Mr Shand Doesn't matter.

She sits on the garden chair

Mrs Shand I was trying so hard to do them neat. I didn't think I was doing them wrong. I'm sorry. (*Pause*) What do you think he's doing now?

Mr Shand Who?

Mrs Shand Jonathan.

Mr Shand tuts

Mr Shand Dunno.

Mrs Shand I wrote him a letter this morning. I can never think of what to say when I'm there. I think of so much when I'm at home, then when we get there, I can never remember. Are you like that?

He grunts

He's getting better, don't you think? He's more alert now. He registers what you say. I think he must think about it more when we've gone. When it's quiet.

Mr Shand It's quiet when we're there.

Mrs Shand He's never violent. I told you what the warden said. About the other prisoners.

Mr Shand You told me.

Mrs Shand About them being violent.

Mr Shand You told me.

Mrs Shand Jonathan's never like that. He's too quiet natured. He was never a rough boy. Not that he couldn't stick up for himself. (*She smiles faintly to herself and looks across at her husband*) Look at you, you're so grouchy. Why don't you go down that club and patch it up with them? It's almost a month now. Show them you don't care.

No response

They'll be on with something else by now. Just go in and show them that you're still the same man. They liked you before.

Mr Shand That were different.

Mrs Shand I still think you might try. It can't go on forever. They haven't banned you.

Mr Shand It's as good as a ban.

Mrs Shand It isn't. Don't be silly.

Mr Shand I don't want to go there. Did I mention it? No. I don't want to go there any more. (*Slight pause*) They're not my kind of people.

Mrs Shand Don't be ridiculous.

Mr Shand If you want to listen to what they say, you go down there. (*Pause*) Are you going to make yourself useful? There's some weeds to pull.

She starts to pull weeds, R

Mrs Shand I know what you mean. It upsets me you should miss out. I've had the same said to me.

Mr Shand I don't think you have.

Mrs Shand I've been hurt. It's a common thing. What they gain by it I really don't know.

Pause

Mr Shand I heard back from that interview. They said no.

Mrs Shand I thought so. I saw the envelope.

Mr Shand I knew I'd done badly. I couldn't say anything right. Everything I said, he criticized me, like I was wrong. But I wasn't wrong. I can do that job with both arms tied. It was just my line of work. I don't get it. Why do I go like that? I was so calm. I knew I could do the job. I just couldn't answer when he asked me things. Simple things. But I couldn't concentrate. Me mind would wander.

Mrs Shand What did you think about?

Mr Shand I don't know. I don't remember. He'd ask me, maybe, how would I organize three men to do a job. I'd try to explain, I knew it in me mind, I could picture t' job, but I couldn't tell 'im.

Mrs Shand There'll be other jobs. You'll do better next time.

Mr Shand I should've got this job. Maybe I shouldn't aim so high. I've been out of work. I ought to work me way back up.

Mrs Shand I thought you said you could do the job.

Mr Shand Maybe I was wrong. It's been a long time. I'm not so sharp now. I can't think so quick.

Mrs Shand You shouldn't undersell yourself.

Pause

Mr Shand Is it raining?

Mrs Shand No.

Mr Shand Thought I felt summat. It's very grey.

Pause

Mrs Shand Poor David — he'll be roasting now, poor boy. It gets so hot. (*Slight pause*) He's a brave lad. (*Slight pause*) Marian prays for him every day. I pray for him too. But Marian says they all pray, and they say a special prayer for him on Sunday. Isn't that nice?

Mr Shand Very thoughtful.

Mrs Shand I think it's good that they don't forget him. He'll sense it, I'm sure. Every time I pray for him, I know that he receives it. Sometimes I almost hear him. Speaking back to me. Isn't that strange. (*Slight pause*) I think that he speaks to Jonathan.

Mr Shand I'll bet he doesn't speak back.

Pause

Mrs Shand I think you were right about the rain. Shall we be packing up?

Mr Shand Packing up? We've only just started. You've got your anorak, haven't you?

Mrs Shand Oh, Reg — we'll get pneumonia. It's cold.

Mr Shand I'm stopping here. You do what you like.

She stays

Mrs Shand It is cold. We can do it tomorrow.

Mr Shand As I say, do what you like.

Mrs Shand Taskmaster. (*She continues pulling weeds*) I've got a book at home with all my thoughts written in it. If I had it now, I'd put that sometimes I think that you don't care. You're so stern; it worries me. I know you're not one for sentiment, but I think you might be more compassionate.

Mr Shand I've no idea where this is coming from.

Mrs Shand You're putting up this brave front, but one day it'll all catch up with you. You'll wake up one day and realize that you can't hide away your feelings, and then you'll be sorry.

Mr Shand This is good of you, Jean. You make me feel so much better.

Mrs Shand You don't listen to me because you think I don't matter. I just hope I'm still here when you need me.

Mr Shand You're a bloody manic depressive.

Mrs Shand There's a little voice that keeps me going. It's a voice of hope. Whenever I'm feeling especially depressed, I hear these words of reassurance telling me that, whatever it is, it's not going to last forever. Things will change. And if things are going badly, it follows that things will change for the better. It's a little voice inside. Only you're so mean and stern. I know that even if you had a voice like that, you wouldn't listen to it. You're too mean and angry. But I'm ready to be patient with you.

Mr Shand I don't want no patience.

Mrs Shand It's always there.

Mr Shand I wish you'd talk some sense. It's nonsense talk.

Pause

Mrs Shand Did I show you those new tablets? Size of an egg, almost. I

said to him, "I'm not *that* ill, you know". He gives them out like they're
sweets. Reg — are you listening?

Mr Shand As always.

She regards him dubiously

Mrs Shand I told him about the nights. That they're getting slightly
easier.

Mr Shand You're still not sleeping.

Mrs Shand I didn't want him thinking I wasn't trying. Oh, but they are
getting easier. I'm much more calm. I can close things off now. It's
getting better, I'm sure.

Mr Shand Why did he give you more tablets then?

Mrs Shand I don't think he realizes. I'll not take them. He doesn't think
I'm getting better — he says I should've responded more to the last lot.
I don't think he knows what he's doing. He's at sixes and sevens, the
poor boy. He's new.

Pause. Mr Shand is digging, disinterested

Reg, it's cold — let's be finishing, eh?

He sighs impatiently. He continues digging

We can start again tomorrow.

Mr Shand I've got a lot of work to do.

Mrs Shand We can do it tomorrow.

Mr Shand I've got lettuces, them carrots, there's some weeds to pull, and
a cutting to plant.

Mrs Shand (*angrily*) For Christ's sake, Reg, it's not important!

He stares at her, shocked

Black-out

SCENE 2

Jonathan's prison cell. Night

The Lights are tight on Jonathan, lying on his bed, fully clothed. A cassette player is heard. It is Veronica's voice, very emotionally wound up

Veronica's voice "It's getting quite light now. I think there's going to be some people ... maybe you should listen to this just once, as if it were a conversation. (*Slight pause*) I wish I had the nerve to come and see you. But I'll never/see you again."

Jonathan Never ... Never.

Veronica's voice "I don't want to think about you. Because it isn't fair. I've got this terrible pain on the top of my head. I can feel the top of my head, just caving in almost. (*Slight pause*) It's a/ terrible thing. I never felt like this."

Jonathan   ... terrible thing. I never felt like this.

Veronica's voice "You've got to take care, it's really silly, but you've ... (*Slight pause*) I don't have to think of anything that we ever did together, but I can't help it. It all just floods right back. I wish it wouldn't. I've got to stop it. I can't just stop things so suddenly. Things don't happen so suddenly. You can't just change things, in an instant (*Slight pause*) I won't do it."

The silent tape continues to run. Jonathan speaks in a rhythm: a swift and steady pace which he maintains

Jonathan Here I am — right — and my life — it's going on, going smoothly, no problems — Happy; you're happy; there's prospects — no — good prospects. So I settle back — I'm OK — I start to plan things — make it better — move out, move on — I need support — I have you — it's logical — So I'm planning — and I'm happy — and then the promotion — I'm happier still — And I know you will be — I think you will be —

Then the party — everyone there — the next step — and I'm happy — but I'm nervous — because you're there — You're not happy — I'm doubtful — but never mind — there's the future — so I wait —

Then I see you — alone — then I ask you —

Then you tell me. (*Pause*) That was it — so ...

It was the party ... And then ... (*Pause*)

So I have prospects — I have a job — a car —

OK, I have prospects — a job — a car —

He starts to panic

I have prospects — a future — "You have the finest future ahead of you" —

They like me — I'm popular — They tell me —

He stands, moves restlessly, irritated

You can move on — you must build — build — build — build —

So I'm building —

I hear "Move" — so I move — and I work — I work hard — and I'm pushing — to get on — get up — I'm going on — it's going great — I'm very well liked — very popular — I can hardly believe it.

Pause

(*Slower*) I took you to one side and said, "This is what I want for us". I said "us", not "me"; it was always "us". You agreed. We shook hands and we kissed and said "Partners". I remember.

(*Back in pace*) So I work — I've got a job — I'm moving up — a bigger job — I'm feeling happy — that's the thing — and I've got you — that's the thing —

Pause

(*Slower*) The first time ... I went home and cried. I was so happy. I knew, one way or the other, that there was something final about you. How could I not feel something like that when it was clear, and you were so right?

"You can't trust a soul," Dad said.

I loved you more than anything. I said blue for the kitchen, but you said white.

David would wear his uniform, and your sister would catch the flowers, and we'd get them dancing together. We'd be a four then.

He is smiling. He stops and looks about him, baffled, lost. Focus on this for several seconds

(*Finally*) Where do I go? I can't just stop. I've got to move. Got to change — progress. Where's the catch?

Look at this — it's got to stop — I can't have it — it must stop — Is it funny? Should I laugh now? Is it funny? Is it a laugh? I don't get it —

I have a job — a car — I have prospects —

Where are you, then? What is it? — it's me — Why me? —

Veronica — it's got to stop now —

David — I've got a job —

(*Loudly, impatiently*) What's the problem? What do you want now? I've got my prospects —

Pause. He settles down. He sits down, slowly

I just want to know what I'm supposed to do.

I don't get it.

Mum ...

I'm lost.

Black-out

SCENE 3

The Shands' living-room. Afternoon

The room looks particularly neat, polished

But this does not stop Mrs Shand from flitting around hurriedly, plumping cushions, making it perfect. This pantomime continues for a while. Finally, she settles and sits in R armchair. No sooner has she done so when the sound of the front door is heard and she excitedly stands again, dashing to the L door

The L door opens and Mr Shand enters, carrying a suitcase

She looks beyond him and reacts as David, in military uniform, enters the room

She looks at him. He smiles. Silently, she reaches out, pulls him to her, hugs him tightly for a long time

By now Mr Shand has put the case down and he watches them impatiently

Mr Shand Come on, then.

Mrs Shand pulls back from David to look at him. Then she starts to cry and hugs him again

 (*Impatiently*) Oh, bloody 'ell! (*He moves into the room and sits in the R armchair*) I told 'im we'd 'ave scenes. I said, "Wait while your mother sees you."

David releases himself and moves into the room

David Shall we sit down?
Mrs Shand I want to look at you.
David Well, let me come in then. (*He closes the door*)

Mrs Shand moves UC, still looking at David

 It's a long time since I saw this place.
Mrs Shand We've had a tidy-up. I polished round. You look tired.
David I am tired. (*He sits in the L armchair*)
Mrs Shand Oh, David! I can't believe it! (*Her hand goes up to her face.*

She has been crying, and now she sniffs, wipes her eyes) We've had such a time of it. You're home now. (*She still looks at him in disbelief*) Are you hungry?

David Not really.

Mrs Shand Are you sure? I can do you something now.

Mr Shand He's 'ad some chips.

Mrs Shand Oh. Right. Well, there's a roast in for later. You'll be ready for that, won't you?

David smiles. He is tired

I know — a cup of tea. Are we all for that?

David Not for me, thanks.

Mrs Shand Are you sure? It's no trouble.

Mr Shand He doesn't want one. Come and sit down, Jean. We're all right.

Mrs Shand I'm just popping upstairs. I've left my hanky ... All this crying, I'm sure I look a right state!

She moves to the UR door. She looks back at David and smiles before she exits

Silence. David looks across at his father, who is surveying the floor. He looks up gingerly and, after a moment, David makes an encouraging, funny expression. Mr Shand's return gesture is the weakest hint of smiles

Mrs Shand As I said, she's not been so good.

David I've seen her look better.

Mr Shand She plods on. We both do. But it's not nice. There's some evil buggers.

Pause

David You've been keeping busy then?

Mr Shand As I say, I'm still tryin' wi' jobs. But there's not much about. I like to potter round me allotment. Takes me mind off things.

David nods. Pause. Silence. David looks about him and laughs slightly

David I can't believe how different it looks. It seems so small.

Mr Shand It's the same room.

David I know. It just seems smaller. I don't know why.

Silence. David looks at Mr Shand, whose gaze is now firmly rooted on the floor. David's expression shows the surprise and disappointment at the sight of his father. He says nothing

Mrs Shand returns eventually

Mrs Shand We're very quiet.

Mr Shand He were sayin', it looks smaller in here. I said, it's same room.

Mrs Shand It's with being away for so long. Your mind plays tricks, doesn't it? (*Slight pause*) We *could* do with some more space, I suppose. (*She sits on the settee*) Now, how was your journey?

David Not bad. Quite long. A couple of stops.

Mrs Shand I see. I expect you were all glad to be on your way back home. It was hot, wasn't it?

David nods

You've caught the sun. In your face. Hasn't he caught the sun, Reg?

Mr Shand Ay — he has.

Silence

Mrs Shand Did you get my letters?

David Yes, I did. Thanks.

Mrs Shand I'm not a great letter writer but I thought I'd try and write. Keep you informed. We've had a busy time. What with you away and — everything.

She looks across at Mr Shand who sits quietly, emotionless

David How is he?

Mrs Shand (*evasively*) Fine.

David You've been going to see him?

Mrs Shand When we could, yes.

David And how's he coping?

Mrs Shand (*unsure*) All right. (*Firmer*) He's fine. He'll be glad to see you, I'm sure.

Silence

(*A forced chuckle*) There's so much to say, and we can't think of anything!

She looks to Mr Shand, fruitlessly. Silence. Then the telephone starts to ring. Nobody moves

Shall I get it? No, you get it, David. It'll probably be for you. It's probably one of your friends.
Mr Shand One of you get it!
David (*standing*) I'll get it.

As he moves to answer the phone, Mrs Shand glares at her husband in response to his tone. He does not react

(*Into the phone*) Hello? ... Yes, it is...

There is a loud cheer down the phone. David holds it away from his ear, then brings it back

(*A few seconds, then*) I'm fine. ... Yes, I do recognize who it is, yes. (*He covers the receiver; whispering to Mrs Shand*) It's Gerald and Marian. (*Back into the phone*) Yes. ... It was long. A couple of stops. ... Yes. ... (*Pause*) Oh that's nice. Very kind of you, Marian. ... I'm a size forty-two. ... Thank you. ... I'm sorry? ... Oh, I see. Just a minute I can't ... I'm sorry? ... No, it wasn't that, I'm just ... Could you say that again, please? ... No, not you, Gerald. ... No. ... Oh, I see. (*He laughs politely*) That's right, Gerald. (*He rolls his eyes. Pause*) What? ... Yes, she's here. ... No. ...

Mrs Shand stands

No, she's just here, if you want a word. ... (*Enunciating*) Just here. ... Is this a bad line? ... Hello? ... Excuse me ... Excuse ... (*He tuts and holds the phone away. To Mrs Shand*) Will you speak to them?

Mrs Shand goes to the phone

(*He checks the phone again*) They're arguing. Gerald's on the upstairs phone. He won't put it down. (*He hands the phone to Mrs Shand*)

Mrs Shand Hello, Marian. ... (*She waits*) Hello. Hello, Marian. ... Yes, it's me. ... He's gone off. He's put me on. ... No. He says he'll speak to you another time. ...

David tuts

He's fine. He's looking really well. ... Yes. ... (*Pause*) Oh, I see. Well look ... Look, Marian, would you mind if I ... Yes. ... Look, Marian, how's about if we discuss this another time. ... I am interested, the church does a wonderful job, I'm just saying why don't you tell me this another time, all right? ... Right. ... Yes, I'll tell him that. ... Yes. ... OK, Marian. ... Right, bye, bye. ... (*Pause*) OK, bye, Marian. ... Yes. ... Bye, Marian. ... (*Pause. Firmly*) Goodbye. (*She puts the phone down*) She does go on. She means well, but she'll talk all day if you let her.

She looks at Mr Shand, who is lifeless, then at David, who appears equally vacant. Pause

So, where were we then?

No reply

Fade slowly to Black-out

SCENE 4

The same

Mrs Shand stands by the sideboard. Mr Shand sits in the R armchair, staring ahead. There are two suitcases by the door

Mr Shand It's stupid. You don't gain anything. Stupid cow.
Mrs Shand You see, that's what's done it.
Mr Shand I don't care what you say. I'm not listening. You're mental. You've got stupid ideas from stupid doctors. I'm not listening to you.
Mrs Shand I wish I could've talked to you about/ it. I'd've sooner talked to you than total strangers.
Mr Shand You're not coming back. I'll lock the door. You think you're coming back, you can sod it.
Mrs Shand You never listened./ You were always too busy.

Mr Shand You've no need to go on about it. I've told you. Shut it! Shut it — you've been told.

Mrs Shand You'll wish you hadn't spoken to me like that.

Mr Shand Belt up.

Pause

Mrs Shand I don't think I'm being unreasonable.

Mr Shand You don't know what to think. You've gone mad. You're worse than that stupid son of yours.

Mrs Shand Anyone'd think he wasn't your son as well.

Mr Shand He's not. This is it — he's had it now. He's a bloody disgrace. He'll never get a civil word from me again. Filthy little bugger. And I don't know why David wastes his time.

Mrs Shand David's gone because he cares.

Mr Shand He's too bloody soft. He wants to toughen up. I thought that bloody war would've toughened him up. He's no better now than when he went. If anything, he's worse. I can't believe this family.

Pause

Mrs Shand I've made you a list. I'll leave it on here. (*She places it on the sideboard*)

Mr Shand You get worse by the minute.

Mrs Shand I think it covers everything.

Mr Shand You've had nothing but patience from me. Not that you bloody deserved it. You don't help yourself. You want to stop being so damned soft. I've no more patience for you.

Mrs Shand I don't know why you should be surprised. I've mentioned it often enough.

Mr Shand Don't think you're bothering me. Sod that. Get gone — see if I care.

Mrs Shand You can't say I didn't warn you.

Pause. Mr Shand remains seriously disgruntled

Mr Shand I'll tell you what it is. It's them bloody neighbours. That's what it is. You're only/ doing it to get away from them.

Mrs Shand The neighbours have got nothing to do with it.

Mr Shand It's 'cause you're ashamed. You know that they talk about you every time you leave that door, so you're runnin' away.

Mrs Shand Don't be ridiculous.

Mr Shand It's Jonathan, and it's David, and it's them soddin' neighbours, but it's not me.

Mrs Shand Is that what you think? It's just as well I'm leaving then.

Mr Shand It doesn't scare me. Them suitcases. Doesn't bother me.

Mrs Shand Good for you.

Mr Shand It's all talk.

Mrs Shand Is it?

Mr Shand We'll see.

Mrs Shand looks at her watch and puts her overcoat on

You'll not get far. Not on a Sunday. It's Sunday, you know.

Mrs Shand I know what day it is, thank you very much.

Mr Shand Think you're smart. There's no buses on a Sunday.

Mrs Shand I know.

Mr Shand Oh. You're wasting your money on a taxi. They'll charge you double for a Sunday. Or maybe it's treble now, I don't know. Where are you going?

No reply

I don't care. You're totally mad. They'll put you away, wherever you go. (*Slight pause*) I saw that letter from your doctor. About drugs. I think it's disgraceful. You'll end up like a delinquent, out on t' streets. This is the end for you. You've had it now.

Pause

I suppose you'll be back round that prison.

Mrs Shand What makes you think that?

Mr Shand You're in league with him.

Mrs Shand I'm trying to help him.

Mr Shand Another waste of time. He won't even talk to you. Just sits there.

Mrs Shand He can hear me.

Mr Shand You ought to be ashamed. You would be ashamed, if you had a shred of decency about you.

Mrs Shand It's his birthday next week.

Mr Shand Huh! He can forget that.

Doorbell

Mrs Shand (*cheerily*) I'll get it.

   She exits to the front door

Mr Shand Bloody visitors. Snoops.
Mrs Shand (*off*) Hallo. You're early. Do you want to come in for a drink?

   Gerald and Marian enter, followed by Mrs Shand

   Sit down. Shall I take your coats?
Marian No; it's all right.
Mrs Shand Sit down. I'll get some tea — kettle's just boiled.

   She exits to the kitchen

Gerald and Marian edge in, wary of Mr Shand, and sit down. Silence

Gerald They're digging that road again. Kept us waiting.

Silence

Marian How's the allotment, Reg?
Mr Shand 'S all right.
Gerald Did you plant those radishes, like I said?
Mr Shand No.
Gerald Oh.
Marian Is David about?
Mr Shand Gone out.
Marian We were hoping to catch him. How is he?
Mr Shand Not so bad. (*He stands, gets his shoes, and starts to put them on*)
Gerald Are you off down the allotment?
Mr Shand Yes.
Gerald What are you on with at the moment?
Mr Shand Lettuces, carrots. All sorts.
Gerald I might have a wander down later.

Mr Shand Please yourself. I can't talk Gerald, I've a lot to do.
Gerald Ah. Maybe next time then.

Mr Shand stands

Mrs Shand emerges from the kitchen with a tray of tea. She stops

Mrs Shand Are you going out?
Mr Shand Get a couple of hours in; before it goes dark.
Mrs Shand I'll be gone, you know.

He stands, says nothing. She puts the tea down. Marian starts to pour

Marian We had ever such a time getting here. They can't leave that one-way system alone.
Mrs Shand Is there anything else you need?

He stands in silence

I've left you a list. There's a phone number on there also, but you know Marian's number, don't you?

Silence

Sure you don't want a cup of tea before you go?

No reply

Marian Have some tea, Reg.

Mr Shand looks at his wife

Mr Shand I don't see why other people should interfere.
Mrs Shand If you're referring to Marian, I rang her. And I'm very grateful to her.
Mr Shand There's some things that should be kept private.
Mrs Shand Sometimes things go too far.
Mr Shand Don't think I'll forget this.
Gerald We're only trying to help.
Mr Shand You were no bloody help when you were needed. When it all

came out, you were nowhere to be seen.

Marian We didn't want to interfere.

Mr Shand You didn't want to know. You were scared for your name. You treated us like dirt.

Mrs Shand That's not true.

Mr Shand (*angrily*) Don't you bloody start! Bloody hypocrite. The first three weeks we got one visit from these. Just while they saw what a state you were in. Then they didn't want to know.

Mrs Shand As a matter of fact I asked them not to visit. I didn't want anyone to see me.

Mr Shand They didn't want to know. If you'd've asked them, they'd've found an excuse.

Gerald That's not right — that's unfair.

Mr Shand No it's not.

Gerald We've done our bit. When Jean rang, we came/ right away. You can't say we don't do our bit.

Mr Shand You weren't welcome. You weren't wanted.

Marian We understand your position, Reg. It's very difficult.

Mr Shand I don't want no bloody sympathy, I just want for you to stop interferin'. Wouldn't be so bad if it was genuine.

Marian How can you say that?

Mr Shand I know it. You're all in it together. You've come here ... (*A sudden pause. He looks at his wife, realizing what is happening*) Jean ... Well what am I supposed to say?

Pause

Mrs Shand I think it's too late.

Pause

Marian Do you want us to wait in the car?

A moment

Mrs Shand (*finally*) No. (*She still looks at her husband*)
Mr Shand Right. (*He moves to leave*) I'm off.

He looks to the visitors and registers their phoney expressions

You're pathetic. (*He looks at Mrs Shand*) The lot of you.

Mr Shand exits R

Silence

Marian I've got the spare room ready; you can stay as long as you like.

Pause

Do you know what you're doing yet?

Mrs Shand shakes her head

There's no hurry. Take your time. Stay with us.
Gerald Has she told you the news? I got a job.
Mrs Shand Really?
Gerald It's the same people. They called me back. Couldn't make the orders on time. So they called me back, see.
Mrs Shand Very nice.
Marian It means there'll be more room round the house during the day.

Gerald looks to her, a little disgruntled

Mrs Shand (*her thoughts elsewhere*) He pretends not to. But he knows what it's about.
Marian Yes.
Mrs Shand He'll see about it when I've gone.
Gerald I'm on reduced hours now. And slightly less pay.
Marian I think you're doing the right thing.
Mrs Shand Do you?
Marian If that's what he's like.
Mrs Shand Oh, that was nothing. He's been ranting, raving, thinks it's all my fault.
Marian No.
Mrs Shand It's all got a little bit out of hand.
Marian Well, you're welcome to stay with us for as long as you like.
Gerald Free of charge.
Mrs Shand Thank you.

Pause

Gerald I find it hard to believe it's the same man. He never was very cheerful, but it's a bit much when he's like that. I never did like him much. I always said, didn't I?

Marian We thought things were getting better.

Mrs Shand Not really.

Marian When we last spoke, it seemed to be getting better. He was taking you to the seaside.

Mrs Shand We didn't go.

Marian I must admit, I was a little surprised. We thought things were on the mend. I mean, you can't ignore what's happened, but I thought you were together on it. Men are bastards.

All three are shocked by this

David enters L. *He looks drained, tired. His smile to them is faint and forced*

David! (*She stands and goes to hug him*)

Gerald Welcome home, young man. I want to hear all about it.

David Hallo, Marian. How are you?

Marian Look at you — you've not been sleeping. What are these? Big dark bags.

Mrs Shand How was it?

David (*too forced*) Fine.

Marian I hope you'll make a point of catching up on all that sleep missed. We've heard all about you. There was an article ...

David Yes.

Gerald She bought three copies.

Marian I kept all the cuttings. I've got a big thick scrapbook full. I'll show it to you, and you can tell me the stories.

Mrs Shand Did he see you?

David I'll tell you later.

Marian See who? Did who see you?

Pause

Oh, David, is that where you've been? You're too good. Your first

Sunday back.

Gerald I don't get it.

Marian He's been to visit his brother. On his first Sunday back.

Mrs Shand David, there's some tea here. Why don't you come and sit down.

Gerald He's been to see Jonathan? What for?

He is glared at for this

Marian And how was he, David?

David I don't really feel like talking just now.

Mrs Shand Have some tea. (*She hands him a cup*)

David It's very tiring.

Gerald You've been to the prison? On your first Sunday back?

Marian Isn't he an angel?

Mrs Shand Was he talking?

David Oh yes.

Mrs Shand What did he say?

David Plenty.

Mrs Shand Was he pleased to see you?

No reply

Oh. You didn't fight, did you?

David I'll tell you later.

Marian We've heard he's been very difficult.

David (*sharply*) Is it surprising?

Marian No.

Mrs Shand Drink your tea, David. Calm down.

David He's ill, you know.

Mrs Shand I know.

David He needs support, and he needs help.

Mrs Shand I know.

David You've hardly been to see him.

Mrs Shand We have.

David When?

Mrs Shand Last week.

David Well ... (*To the others*) Did you go?

They look at him, shocked

You don't like to.

Marian Think of what he did.

David I know what he did. I've just seen him.

Gerald Nobody could condone what he did. It's too terrible for words.

David He killed a man.

They are shocked

Marian I think I must be old-fashioned, I find all this very difficult.

David It's simple enough.

Gerald It's a wicked business. I don't think we should talk about it.

David If you stop trying to complicate matters.

Gerald I don't think we're doing that.

David I think you are. (*Pause*) What do you think of me?

Gerald What's that?

David How do I compare with Jonathan?

Gerald There is no comparison.

David Oh, I think we could work on one.

Gerald He's a different kind of person. It's a different thing.

David What is?

Pause

Do you realize what I've been doing?

No reply

Do you realize what I've done?

Silence

Marian I was thinking we might get on the road. I don't like driving in the dark.

No reply

Is there anything else to pack?

Mrs Shand No. The cases are there. Would you mind if I had a word alone with David?

Marian We'll wait in the car. Gerald.

She stands. He stands

Gerald, can you manage those cases?

Gerald hesitates to answer

David I'll bring them.
Marian Oh, all right. No problem then. We'll wait in the car. The red one, Jean.
Mrs Shand OK.
Marian Come on, Gerald. Let's make a move now, shall we.
Gerald (*feebly*) See you later, David.

No reply

Gerald and Marian exit

Brief silence

David It surprises me you chose them. Is there no-one else?
Mrs Shand No. (*Pause*) He spoke to you then. I told you what he's like. I don't know how to take him. (*Pause*) Did you tell him about me?
David No.
Mrs Shand What did you talk about?
David Nothing.
Mrs Shand Nothing?
David I hardly said anything. He wasn't in the mood to listen.

Pause

I'm going back. I don't care if it takes the next ten years. I'm going back till I get him to hear me. And then I'm going to tell him precisely what I think.
Mrs Shand And what *do* you think?

Pause

David I think that he needs me ...
Mrs Shand And ...?

No reply. Long pause

David (*standing*) I'll take your cases.

Mrs Shand I have to do this, David. I have to do something — you do understand? Otherwise ... It's going to go on forever.

David I think that you're doing the right thing.

Mrs Shand Do you?

David Yes. I think that you're right. You have to do something.

He lifts the cases and moves to exit R

Black-out

SCENE 5

The Prison Room. A visit several weeks later

Bright Lights come up on David and Jonathan, as in the Prologue

Jonathan No sharp objects. No knives, bullets, toys and games. Don't bring things. Don't ... don't ... you'll annoy them!

David What's the matter?

Jonathan (*pointing at the door*) We've got men who keep the noise down. Don't yell. Keep quiet. Keep it down, lads, come on now let's keep it down. (*Suddenly*) Alastair Angry in seventy-two ... Alastair Angry ...

David What?

Jonathan (*shouting*) ... KILLED HIMSELF!!

Pause

We've got madmen all around us. Do you realize this is the maximum high security top security highest mental metal prison in all the whole of England? And/ this is the toughest. Of all England.

David It's not the worst. There are others.

Pause

Jonathan Took a knife in breakfast canteen and hid it in his boot. Then he took it out at two in the morning and sliced away and shouted at us all, 'cause he still had things to say, but he floated away too quick and he didn't have time to say it.

I knew what he wanted to say. He wanted to tell us what it's like when you're dead. He found it out. He was trying to tell us. But he floated away. He got dragged out in a white sheet. They said, "Bloody bloody bloody mess". He's only painted his bloody cell red.

Frigging smelly, I should say!

Filthy's what they thought, but really it was beautiful, 'cause it was natural. That's what they don't get. But I get it. It's natural. What's the problem? They've all got blood to spill. It's all right really.

David I still know you, Jonathan. I know what you're doing.

Jonathan We've got vermin in the khazi. It's out there! Cross your legs, lads!

David laughs, exasperated

David If I stopped coming, you'd only think you'd won. So I keep coming; almost to spite you. You can only keep this up/ for so long.

Jonathan If Angus is in there, he whistles. I wait for him to stop. If he stops whistling, if he stops, then he's been got. He doesn't even mind. He wants to be got.

David I know from the warden that you know how to behave. Once the visitors have gone, you go right/ back to being normal.

Jonathan And it's not just him because I'd quite like to be got too. I know I've never seen it, but I know it's there! Killer rat in the khazi — what a way to go! (*He laughs*)

David I remember when you were a boy, at night, you were always too frightened to use the bathroom. You thought that there were monsters in there.

Slight pause. Jonathan deliberately focuses away from him

Dad told you not to be silly. I was the one who had to go in and put the light on for you. Do you remember that? It's not all that long ago.

Pause. Jonathan is rocking on his chair

Jonathan This week's viewer's question comes from Mister Anal Retention of Accrington, Lancashire, who asks: How many times a day

does Angus use the Khazi? Thank you for your question, Mister
Retention, your tie is in the post.

David Yes; you're trying hard today. It's definitely one of your better
days. (*Slight pause*) How's the writing? The warden says he found an
exercise book of stories you'd ——

Jonathan We've got serial killers of every sort here. A man to suit every
requirement. Hatchets, screwdrivers, shotguns, hands, feet, hair, teeth
...

David I heard they were very good, these stories. I wondered if maybe
you'd let me read them. Can I read them? Would you let me?

Pause

What do you write about? Anything in particular?

No reply

Well actually the warden told me. He said you write about adventures.
Children on adventures, making things up, playing at being heroes.
Sounds familiar.

Jonathan We're surrounded by it. Bastards who know what's best for us.

David I don't mind you not answering me. It doesn't bother me. So long
as you listen, and I know that you're listening, 'cause you never were
much good at pretending. Oh, you're trying hard, pretending, but I'm
very sorry ——

*In a swift movement, Jonathan grabs his chair, lifts it, and smashes it to
the ground, yelling angrily. He kicks at it. Then he stops, and stands still,
breathing heavily*

Jonathan Don't nobody be put off now. I am a very mild man. I'm just
a little confused.

Silence. He turns to David

I smash a bottle and a little old man who's doing six times life says, "why
do you do it?" I say, "I don't know why, and if I did know why I wouldn't
tell you, you old weasel-face."

David I know why you break things.

Jonathan And then I say that maybe I do know why. I break things 'cause they're no good and they're there. They shouldn't be there if they're no good. They deserve to be broken. Bastard chair. (*He kicks at the chair*) It's just a shitty wooden chair. (*He kicks it*)

David It is. I couldn't agree more.

Slight pause

Jonathan If there's any justice she'll be dead and buried now. I wanted her crying but that's no good, I want her dead and buried with a metal spike in through her eye and I'd do it myself, and don't think I wouldn't.

Pause

"I can't think of things we did," she said.
David You hurt her too.

Jonathan looks at him and then turns away

Jonathan (*softly*) I've still got a knife.

David is shocked

David Where is it?

Jonathan smirks, knowingly

Jonathan People only get what they deserve. Isn't that true?
David (*earnestly*) Yes.

Pause. Jonathan is feeling uncomfortable, threatened

Jonathan (*suddenly, impatiently*) I've got to get out. I've got things, there are things, I've got, to do./I've got things ... there are things ... (*He looks about him as if searching for the way out*)
David Don't go yet. What about the news? Dad's got a job interview.

Jonathan walks away, towards the L exit

He keeps practising what to say. He's very determined.
Jonathan There's a tournament now and I'm all set to win, it's a certainty I'll win, all set.
David (*trying*) Mum's still at Marian's. She rings him on a Sunday. She

says she'll not go back but at least they're speaking now. It's getting
better.

Jonathan Angus is a bastard. He's got my book. I've got tactics and he
nicks the book from right on my table. He dies, Angus.

David (*losing momentum*) I don't think there's anything else. Mum sends
her love. She says to wear your scarf when you're out in the yard. You
will remember?

Jonathan Fat Angus. He's fat, Angus.

A long pause

David Why won't you listen? Why?

Jonathan paces, his attention elsewhere

What's the matter with you? Do you want me to hate you? Is that it? All
right then, I hate you. All right?

Jonathan still paces

The more that I think about you, the more I give up. And still I come. For
three weeks I come here. Three weeks, and all I get is "Angus is a bastard
— I've got a tournament". Are you punishing me, Jonathan? Is that it?
(*Sadly*) I think you are.

Pause

Why do I come here? Why do I waste my time? Jonathan? — listen to
me! (*He moves towards Jonathan*) I want to help you. I'm here because
I care. Oh, sod this, I'm sick of saying it. (*He looks straight at Jonathan*)
Look at you — you're pathetic. Parading around, self-pitying. Mum's
crying, Dad gets spat at in the street, and here's you. Poor sad lonely you.
No-one understands you. (*Slight pause*) Do you really think you're the
only one? Here's how it is: you killed a man. You killed him, you got
locked up for it. He had a weak heart, they cut the sentence, but it was
you who did it. (*Slight pause*) What's so bad about that? You think
you're hard done by? Think it's unfair? And nobody understands you.

Pause

Were you forced to do it? Were you ordered? (*Angrily*) What about me?

Pause

You feel guilty. You know what you did, but still you can't get close enough to believe it. You need to be punished, you need to suffer, but this punishment, it's not enough. There's still the thought, the image, of the terrible thing you did. (*Slight pause*) People don't know. (*Slight pause*) They tell you what you are ... (*Slight pause*) You know that they're wrong but how can they know when it isn't them? You know what you are. You know what you did. You hear it and see it. (*Slight pause*) Everything you were is gone. And in its place, that one act. The taking of a life. That's it. You're a killer. And it's always going to be there. Until the day you die. (*Slight pause*) Am I right, brother? Is that how you feel?

Jonathan stares at him, his face bearing an expression of relief and sudden understanding. Then, slowly, he extends a hand and takes hold of David's arm. He pulls David to him and the two brothers embrace

Fade to Black-out

CURTAIN

FURNITURE AND PROPERTY LIST

ACT I
PROLOGUE

On stage: Table
Two chairs

SCENE 1

On stage: Large table. *On it*: buffet food, including cheese sandwiches,
a white iced cake with candles, a bowl and packet of crisps,
paper plates, box of matches, cake-knife
Settee. *On it*: cushions
Two armchairs
Model airplane for **Mr Shand**
Sideboard. *On it*: glasses, bottles of wine. *In it*: bottle of wine
Glasses of wine for **Gerald**, **Marian** and **Veronica**
TV
Tape/record player
Tapes/records
Coffee table
Telephone
Tea towel for **Mrs Shand**
Mr Shand's shoes

Personal: **Mrs Shand**: wrist-watch (worn throughout)
Gerald: wrist-watch (worn throughout)

SCENE 2

Set: Mug of tea, half-eaten sandwich on a plate for **Mrs Shand**

SCENE 3

On stage: Gate

SCENE 4

On stage: Two white tables
               Three chairs

Off stage: Cup of coffee (**Waitress**)

Personal: **Waitress**: cloth, notepad, pen
               Veronica: audio-cassette in pocket
               Mrs Shand: handbag

SCENE 5

On stage: Nil

ACT II

SCENE 1

On stage: Vegetable beds with soil. *In* R *patch*: weeds
               Garden chair
               Garden fork for **Mr Shand**
               Packet of carrot seeds for **Mrs Shand**

SCENE 2

On stage: Bed. *On it*: pillow, bedclothes, cassette player

SCENE 3

On stage:	Large table
	Settee. *On it*:cushions
	Two armchairs
	Sideboard
	TV
	Tape/record player
	Tapes/records
	Coffee table
	Telephone
Off stage:	Suitcase (**Mr Shand**)

SCENE 4

Re-set:	Suitcase by door
Set:	Second suitcase by door
	Mrs Shand's overcoat and handbag on settee
	Mr Shand's shoes
Off stage:	Tray of tea (**Mrs Shand**)
Personal:	**Mrs Shand**: list

SCENE 5

On stage:	Table
	Two chairs

LIGHTING PLOT

Property fittings required: nil

Interior and exterior settings

ACT I, Prologue. Prison room

To open: Bright lighting

Cue 1	**Jonathan** moves quickly to L side of room *Black-out*	(Page 2)

ACT I, Scene 1. Living-room

To open: General lighting

Cue 2	**Veronica** cries *Fade to black-out*	(Page 20)

ACT I, Scene 2. Living-room

To open: Virtual darkness

Cue 3	**Mrs Shand** switches on the kitchen light *Snap on light spill from kitchen*	(Page 25)
Cue 4	**David**: "It's like a game." *Snap off light spill from kitchen*	(Page 25)
Cue 5	**David**: "... in all my life." *Fade to black-out*	(Page 26)

ACT I, SCENE 3. Street

To open: Exterior evening effect

Cue 6   **Jonathan** runs off   (Page 27)
           Fade to black-out

ACT I, SCENE 4. Park café

To open: Rich blue daylight

Cue 7   **Mrs Shand** exits L   (Page 33)
           Fade to black-out

ACT I, SCENE 5

To open: Spotlight on **Mrs Shand**

Cue 8   **Mrs Shand**: "That was it."   (Page 33)
           Black-out

ACT II, SCENE 1. Allotment

To open: General lighting

Cue 9   **Mr Shand** stares at her, shocked   (Page 41)
           Black-out

ACT II, SCENE 2. Prison cell

To open: Spotlight on **Jonathan**

Cue 10   **Jonathan**: "I'm lost"   (Page 44)
           Black-out

ACT II, SCENE 3. Living-room

To open: General afternoon lighting

Cue 11   **Mrs Shand**: "So where were we then? " No reply   (Page 49)
          Slow fade to black-out

ACT II, SCENE 4. Living-room

To open: General lighting

Cue 12   **David** moves to exit R   (Page 60)
          Black-out

ACT II, SCENE 5. Prison room

To open: Bright general lighting

Cue 13   The two brothers embrace   (Page 65)
          Fade to black-out

MADE AND PRINTED IN GREAT BRITAIN BY
LATIMER TREND & COMPANY LTD PLYMOUTH
MADE IN ENGLAND

EFFECTS PLOT

ACT I

Cue 1   To open SCENE 1   (Page 2)
Convivial music from tape/record player

Cue 2   **David** changes the music   (Page 7)
Change music

Cue 3   **David** changes the music   (Page 15)
Change music

Cue 4   **Jonathan** turns the music off   (Page 17)
Cut music

Cue 5   To open SCENE 4   (Page 28)
Birdsong, continue throughout scene

ACT II

Cue 6   To open SCENE 2   (Page 41)
Veronica's *voice on tape as script page 42*

Cue 7   **Mrs Shand** looks to **Mr Shand**, fruitlessly. .   (Page 48)
Telephone rings

Cue 8   **Mr Shand**: "He can forget that."   (Page 52)
Doorbell